Contents

Some words are shown in bold, **like this**. You can find out
what they mean by looking in the glossary.

What Is a Grassland Food Web?

Plants, animals, and other living things rely on each other for life. This is because all **organisms** eat and are eaten by other organisms. For example, in a grassland **habitat**, crickets eat grass and are then eaten by mice. When living things die and rot, other organisms such as insects eat them. If you draw lines between the organisms that eat each other, you create a diagram called a food web. It is called a web because it looks like a very tangled spider's web! The arrows lead from the food to the animal that eats it.

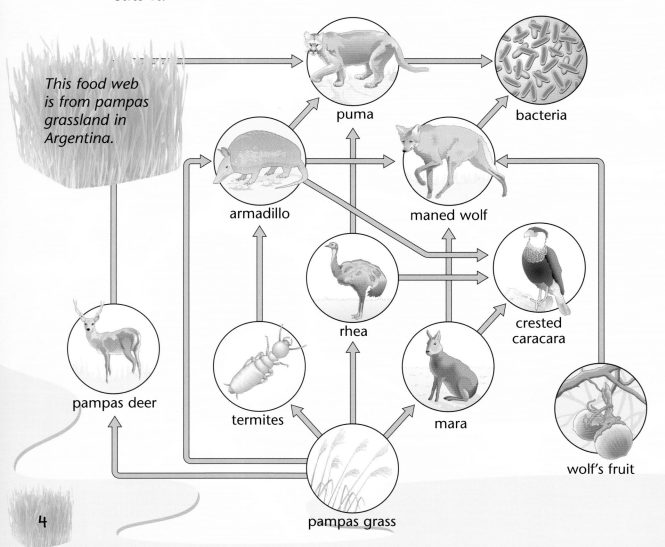

This food web is from pampas grassland in Argentina.

puma

bacteria

armadillo

maned wolf

rhea

crested caracara

pampas deer

termites

mara

wolf's fruit

pampas grass

Food Webs

Grassland Food Chains

Louise and Richard Spilsbury

Heinemann Library
Chicago, Illinois

Chicago, Illinois

Customer Service   888–454–2279

Visit our website at www.heinemannlibrary.com

Photo research by Ruth Blair and Ginny Stroud-Lewis
Designed by Jo Hinton-Malivoire and AMR
Printed in China by WKT Company Limited.

09 08 07 06 05
10 9 8 7 6 5 4 3 2 1

Library of Congress Cataloging-in-Publication Data
Spilsbury, Louise.
  Grassland food chains / Louise Spilsbury and Richard Spilsbury.
      v. cm. — (Food webs)
  Includes bibliographical references (p.   ).
  Contents: What is a grassland food web? — What is a grassland food chain? — What is a producer? — What is a primary consumer? — What is a secondary consumer? — How are grassland food chains different in different places? — What happens to a food web when a food chain breaks down? — How can we protect grassland habitats and food chains?
  ISBN 1-4034-5860-X (lib. bdg.) — ISBN 1-4034-5867-7 (pbk.)
  1. Grassland ecology—Juvenile literature. 2. Food chains (Ecology)—Juvenile literature. [1. Grassland ecology. 2. Food chains (Ecology) 3. Ecology.] I. Spilsbury, Richard, 1963- . II. Title. III. Series.
  QH541.5.P7S67 2004
  577.4—dc22

                              2003026194

Acknowledgments
The author and publisher are grateful to the following for permission to reproduce copyright material: Alamy p. **14**; Corbis pp. **5** (Paul A. Souders), **7** (William Manning), **8** (Joe McDonald), **10** (Craig Lovell), **11** (Galen Rowell), **12**, **27** (RF), **13** (Lynda Richardson), **16** (Yann Arthus-Bertrand), **17** (Tony Wharton/ Frank Lane Picture Agency), **23** (Darrell Gulin), **24** (Wolfgang Kaehler), **26** (Patrick Robert), p. **25**; NHPA pp. **15** (Ann and Steve Toon), **18** (Stephen Dalton), **22** (Martin Harvey).

Cover photograph of a cheetah chasing a young gazelle reproduced with permission of NHPA/Christophe Ratier.

Illustrations by Words and Publications.

The publisher would like to thank Dr Dennis Radabaugh of the Department of Zoology at Ohio Wesleyan University for his comments in the preparation of this book.

Every effort has been made to contact copyright holders of any material reproduced in this book. Any omissions will be rectified in subsequent printings if notice is given to the publisher.

What are grassland habitats like?

Grasslands are large open spaces where the soil is too poor or the weather too dry for trees and many other plants to grow. Instead, tough wild grasses take over the land. Some grasslands were created by people when they cut down forests. Farm animals, such as sheep and cows, keep the forest from coming back by eating plants before they can grow tall.

Tropical grasslands are called savannas. These grasslands are hot all year, and get only short bursts of rain. Savannas have scattered trees and shrubs as well as grasses. Some grasslands grow in **temperate** areas that have hot summers and cold winters. These have fewer trees than the savannas. They are called prairies in the United States, pampas in Argentina, and steppes in Asia.

The tall grasses of the African savanna provide cover for hunters, such as this cheetah.

5

What Is a Grassland Food Chain?

Food webs are made up of a series of simple interlocking food chains. Food chains show the **organisms** that eat each other as links in a single chain. They follow the movement of **nutrients** and **energy** as these pass from one link to another.

Most living things are part of more than one food chain because they eat or are eaten by more than one kind of organism. This makes them part of a more complex food web. A system like this is safer for the organisms within it. If an animal relied on only one food source and that food supply ran out, the animal would starve.

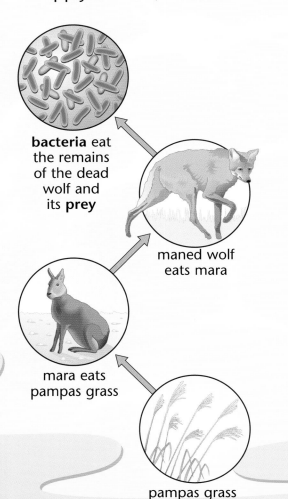

bacteria eat the remains of the dead wolf and its **prey**

maned wolf eats mara

mara eats pampas grass

pampas grass

This is a diagram of a grassland food chain. The arrows show which way the energy moves. Some energy is lost as it passes from one link in the chain to the next.

In the United States, flowers such as these goldenrods and purple blazing stars grow among the grasses in the prairies.

Starting the chain

The Sun is the source of energy for all organisms in the world. Most food chains start with plants because these can trap some of the energy in sunlight in their leaves. They use it to make food in a process called **photosynthesis**. These foods, along with nutrients taken up through their roots, allow plants to grow and make new plants.

Animals cannot make their own food, so some get the energy and nutrients they need by eating plant parts. In grassland **habitats**, bees and butterflies feed on nectar from flowers, while caterpillars, beetles, and grasshoppers munch leaves. Other animals get energy by eating different animals. As the animals feed, energy flows through the food chain and through the habitat.

Making the chain

Food chains usually start with a plant **producer**. Plants are called producers because they make, or produce, food. Animals have to eat other **organisms** to get the **energy** they need, so they are called **consumers**.

Animals that eat only plants are known as **herbivores**. In food chains, herbivores are called **primary consumers**, because they eat the producers. **Carnivores** are animals that eat other animals, such as snakes. They are known as **secondary consumers**. Secondary consumers may eat both primary consumers (the herbivores) and other secondary consumers. Animals that eat both plants and other animals are called **omnivores.** They are primary and secondary consumers.

Copperhead snakes are carnivores, or secondary consumers. This one is eating a deer mouse.

There are always more producers than primary consumers in food chains, and more primary consumers than secondary consumers.

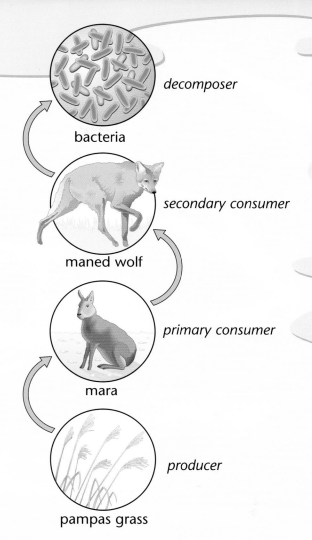

decomposer

bacteria

secondary consumer

maned wolf

primary consumer

mara

producer

pampas grass

More links in the chain

When plants and animals die, other organisms can still use the energy stored in their bodies. **Scavengers** eat the dead remains of other animals. Jackals and white-backed vultures are two grassland scavengers. **Decomposers** such as **bacteria** and **fungi** feed on any dead remains not taken by scavengers. Decomposers break down the remains into tiny pieces. They eat some of them, and other pieces get washed into the soil. Plants take in these soil **nutrients** through their roots, and so the food chain begins again.

Without **decomposers**, the other **organisms** in a **habitat** would eventually die out. Only decomposers can break down dead organisms and their waste into a form that plant **producers** can use to create new supplies of **energy**.

Breaking the chain

If some organisms in a food web die out, it can be deadly for other organisms in the web. Sometimes natural events can break the links in a food chain. Fire is an important part of grassland life. It can destroy all the grass, shrubs, and trees in an area very quickly. The animals that usually eat the plants may then starve and die. This means that the **carnivores** that eat those animals will have less food to eat, too.

*These vulture **scavengers** are feeding on the body of a dead zebra in Tanzania, Africa.*

Which Producers Live in Grasslands?

Grasses are the main producers in grassland food chains, but trees are also important producers in savanna habitats.

Grasses

There are different kinds of grasses in different grassland habitats—such as pampas grass in the Argentinean pampas and feather grass on the Asian steppe—but they all share similar features. The feature that makes them so successful is their ability to live through long periods without rain. This is why grasses are found all over the world. Grasses grow quickly and soon produce seeds. Grass plants are **pollinated** and their seeds are carried by the wind, so they spread over a wide area. In some grasslands, colorful wildflowers grow among the grasses.

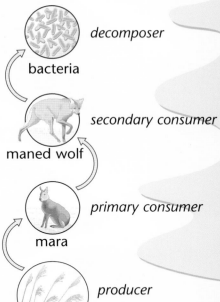

decomposer
bacteria

secondary consumer
maned wolf

primary consumer
mara

producer
pampas grass

On the flat plains of Montana, grasses dotted with flowers cover the land.

Tropical grassland trees

Tropical grassland trees are specially suited to survive the dry, hot **climate**. Many lose their leaves in the dry season and burst into life in the wet season. Some, such as euphorbias and acacias, store water in their tough stems. Acacia trees have thorns to stop animals from eating their leaves and shoots. Some euphorbias contain a bad-tasting milky sap that most hungry animals do not like!

These acacias are the most common trees in the African savanna.

Breaking the Chain: Producers

In parts of the North American prairie, the **larvae** of monarch butterflies feed on milkweed leaves that are poisonous to most insects. The buildup of poison in the larvae and later the adult makes the butterflies poisonous and protects them from being eaten by birds. When farmers burn or cut down these unwanted milkweed plants, many monarch butterflies die, too.

Which Primary Consumers Live in Grasslands?

Insects are the main **primary consumers** in many grasslands. Lots of crickets, locusts, grasshoppers, and many kinds of beetles eat parts of plants. Although insect jaws are small, they are strong and can bite through leaves, stems, and seeds. Grassland insects use wings to fly or long legs to jump from plant to plant to find a meal.

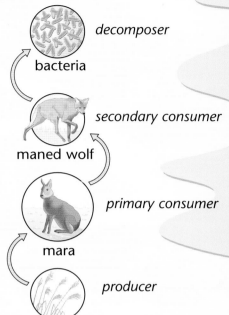

decomposer

bacteria

secondary consumer

maned wolf

primary consumer

mara

producer

pampas grass

Other small grassland animals

Many birds also eat parts of plants. Prairie chickens feed on leaves, fruit, and seeds. Many small grassland **herbivores** live in underground burrows, safe from **predators** and fires. On prairies, prairie dogs eat plant seeds, roots, leaves, flowers, and fruits. Gophers and mole rats dig tunnels to eat roots and other underground plant parts. The long-legged and large-eared jackrabbit feeds, or **grazes**, on grass.

Birds such as this American goldfinch feed on the seeds of grassland flowers.

13

Large grassland herbivores

There are many large grassland **herbivores**. These **primary consumers** usually live and feed in herds. Some members of the group watch for **predators** while the others feed. Some, such as bison and antelopes, have extra stomach chambers that help them break down tough, chewy grasses more fully. Others, like zebras and white rhinos, do not have these. They have to eat even more grass to get enough **nutrients** from it to survive.

In **tropical** grasslands, some large herbivores also eat tree parts. Giraffes and black rhinos eat leaves, buds, and fruit from acacia trees. They use long tongues to snatch leaves from among the thorns of acacias. Elephants strip bark from trees with their trunks, or push them over to eat their leaves and fruit. They pass the food from their trunks into their mouths.

This giraffe is eating from an acacia tree in Kenya, Africa.

Which Secondary Consumers Live in Grasslands?

Carnivores, omnivores, and scavengers are all secondary consumers. Grassland secondary consumers have a variety of ways to find their food. Snakes such as puff adders have little pits on their heads that can sense heat. These help them to catch warm-bodied rodents at night. Nile crocodiles lie in wait at some grassland water holes, ready to catch animals that come to drink there.

decomposer
bacteria

secondary consumer
maned wolf

primary consumer
mara

producer
pampas grass

Bird life

Many grassland birds are also secondary consumers. The red-billed oxpecker hitches a ride on the backs of large grazing animals such as buffalo. It eats parasites called ticks that bite through the bisons' skin and feed on their blood. Birds of prey such as the steppe eagle fly over grassland waiting for animals such as hamsters and voles to come out of their burrows.

Secretary birds often hunt snakes and lizards, but this one has caught a rodent.

Dogs, cats, and scavengers

Grassland dogs include African wild dogs, maned wolves, and dingoes. They eat **prey** such as **rodents**, rabbits, antelope, and zebra. On the savanna, lions, leopards, and cheetahs hunt for food. A large animal such as an antelope can provide them with enough food for several days. Grassland **scavengers** include birds such as vultures and marabou storks, and animals such as brown hyenas. Hyenas sometimes chase lions away from their kills.

Lions work in teams to bring down prey larger than themselves.

Breaking the Chain: Secondary Consumers

In the United States, farmers once poisoned prairie dogs because they mistakenly believed that these animals' burrows were a hazard for cattle and that the prairie dogs competed with cattle for grass. Poisoning and shooting reduced prairie dog populations by 90 percent and made the black-footed ferret, an animal that eats prairie dogs, an **endangered species**.

Which Decomposers Live in Grasslands?

Grassland **decomposers** include **bacteria** and **fungi**. They live in the soil in open grasslands, because dead animals and plants and their waste usually end up there.

Bacteria and fungi

Bacteria and fungi break down large amounts of dead matter and waste in grassland **habitats**. They cannot "eat" food as animals do. They feed by releasing chemicals called enzymes into the dead animal or plant. The enzymes break down the dead body into liquid **nutrients**. Bacteria or fungi then take in some of these nutrients to feed. The rest washes into the ground, making a rich soil where grasses and other plants can grow.

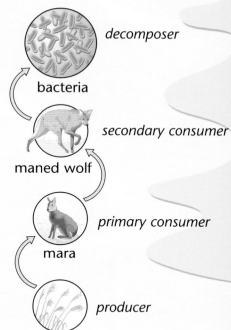

decomposer

bacteria

secondary consumer

maned wolf

primary consumer

mara

producer

pampas grass

Mushrooms and toadstools are the parts of a fungus that produce tiny, seedlike spores. The main part of the fungus is a network of tiny threads that run through the soil.

Animals that help decomposers

When some animals eat dead **organisms**, they help break them down into smaller bits that **decomposers** can use. These mini-**scavengers** include insects and worms.

Termites are antlike insects that live in groups in earth nests up to 33 feet (10 meters) high. They feed mainly on dead wood and plants. This is useful because plants contain cellulose, and this substance is hard for any other insects to break down.

The small, flat carrion beetle finds dead animals by smell. It buries the bodies of small animals and lays eggs on them. When the **larvae** hatch out of the eggs, they can feed on the body.

Grassland soil contains millions of very tiny worms called nematodes. Some are **parasites** on plants, but most are helpful to the soil. They feed on **bacteria**, **fungi**, or other nematodes, and let **nutrients** out into the soil as waste.

The maggots that feed on dead animals are the larvae of flies. Adult flies lay their eggs in a dead animal, and the larvae that hatch out feed on its flesh.

How Are Grassland Food Chains Different in Different Places?

Food chains and webs can be very different from one grassland to another. These are three important grasslands.

The African savanna

The biggest **tropical** grassland in the world is the savanna, stretching from southern Africa up to the Sahara desert in the north. In addition to the patches of grass that grow here, there are areas of thorny bushes and open woodland.

Grasses here provide food for huge herds of gnus and zebras. Giraffes feed on the tallest acacia trees, and black rhinos nibble smaller bushes. African wild dogs hunt in large groups to bring down large **herbivores** such as gnus. Lions hide in the grass as they creep up on their **prey**. Other smaller savanna **primary consumers** include insects. These are eaten by **secondary consumers** such as lizards and meerkats.

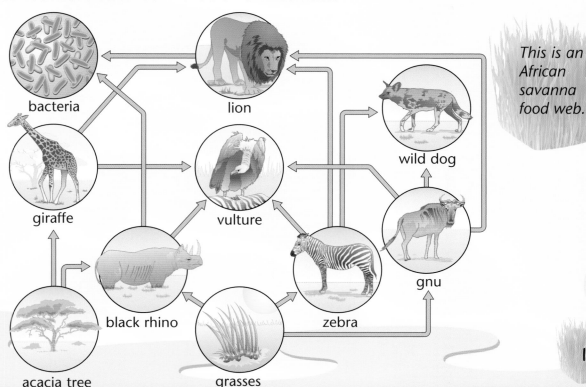

bacteria

lion

wild dog

giraffe

vulture

gnu

black rhino

zebra

acacia tree

grasses

This is an African savanna food web.

19

The North American prairie

Prairie once covered the flat land in the middle of North America from Canada down to Texas. Much of this area is now farmland. The main prairie **producers** are grasses. Big bluestem is one of the tallest at up to 10 feet (about 3 meters) high. The grasses are eaten by grasshoppers, prairie dogs, and bison. Bison are up to 6.5 feet (2 meters) tall and eat 66 pounds (30 kilograms) of plants each day!

Western meadowlarks, prairie chickens, and skink eat insects such as grasshoppers. Rattlesnakes eat a varied diet including lizards, frogs, **rodents**, birds' eggs, chicks, and prairie dogs. Coyotes **scavenge** large animal remains or hunt small **prey** such as prairie dogs. Prairie ants carry seeds and insects back to underground nests to eat.

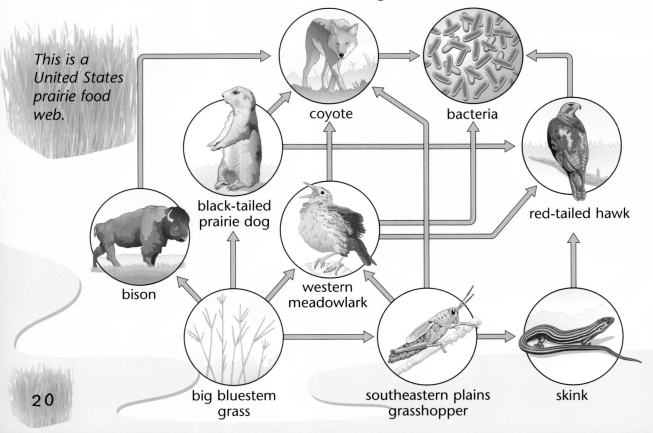

This is a United States prairie food web.

coyote

bacteria

black-tailed prairie dog

red-tailed hawk

bison

western meadowlark

big bluestem grass

southeastern plains grasshopper

skink

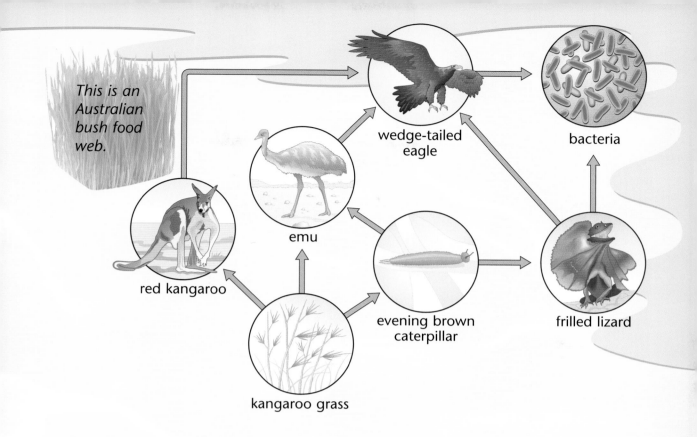

This is an Australian bush food web.

wedge-tailed eagle

bacteria

emu

red kangaroo

evening brown caterpillar

frilled lizard

kangaroo grass

The Australian bush

Bush, a type of dry savanna grassland dotted with trees, stretches across northern and parts of southern Australia. Gum or eucalyptus trees are common here. Koalas are one of the few **herbivores** that can eat the oily leaves of these trees, because they have special **bacteria** in their stomachs to help them break down this food. Some of the largest Australian animals, such as kangaroos and wallabies, feed on low plants such as kangaroo grass.

The emu is a bird that is almost 5 feet (1.5 meters) tall and cannot fly. It eats plants but is also a secondary consumer of insects. The wedge-tailed eagle, a **bird of prey**, hunts striped emu chicks hidden in the bush grasses, and also **mammals** such as kangaroos. The eagle is also the major bush scavenger.

What Happens to a Food Web When a Food Chain Breaks Down?

The food chains and webs in many **habitats** are at risk because of human activities. When something affects one link in a food chain, it can have harmful effects for the chain and other parts of the food web.

Overgrazing

Some grasslands are damaged when too many animals are allowed to **graze** an area, a problem called overgrazing. The grass plants get tugged up by their roots so they cannot grow back. Once the blanket of grass that covered the land is gone, the rich top layer of soil blows away or is washed away by rain. This leaves very dry land where little grows. Overgrazing by wild and farm animals has destroyed many of the grasslands in the world, sometimes even turning them into deserts.

Overgrazing in this part of India has turned what was once grassland into dusty desert.

Areas like this in North America are often called the "breadbaskets of the world" because so much wheat for making bread and other food is grown on land that was once wild prairie.

Habitat destruction

Many wild grassland habitats have disappeared. Huge areas have been changed into crop-growing farmland. Some areas have been taken over by people for building houses, offices, or factories. Others have been taken for parks, playing fields, or golf courses.

Wild prairie grassland once covered a huge area of North America. Since the beginning of the 20th century, most of this land has been plowed to grow another kind of grass—wheat. As more and more of the wild prairie has been lost to farming, more and more grazing animals have died out in the area, including herds of antelopes known as pronghorns. This means that their **predators** in the food chain, such as wolves, have also disappeared from these areas.

In Africa, elephants are an endangered species because people hunt them for their ivory tusks.

Hunting

People hunt and kill grassland animals for many reasons. For example, African rhinos are hunted just for their valuable horns. Long ago in the United States, so many bison on the prairies were killed for their meat and skins that they almost died out completely. In the Australian bush today, thousands of kangaroos are killed each year for their skins. These are often used to make soccer shoes.

Breaking the Chain: Unwanted Additions

When a new link is introduced to food webs, it can cause problems. For example, in the mid-1800s, people took wild rabbits from England to Australia for sport hunting. They spread rapidly and became one of the worst pests in the Australian bush. Rabbits eat so many of the grasses and other plants that they leave little food and shelter for **native** animals. By removing so many plants, they also damage the soil.

How Can We Protect Grassland Food Chains?

Around the world, scientists and **conservation** groups are working to protect the living things in grassland food chains and webs.

Scientists at work

Scientists study **endangered species** of plants and animals to understand how they live, how they fit into grassland food chains and webs, and what they need to survive. For example, in the African savanna, people track rare black rhinos by recognizing and following their footprints. They learn what area the rhinos roam over to find plants to eat. They study how the rhino population changes over time and whether illegal hunting is happening. The scientists can then make suggestions to governments and other people responsible for protecting grasslands.

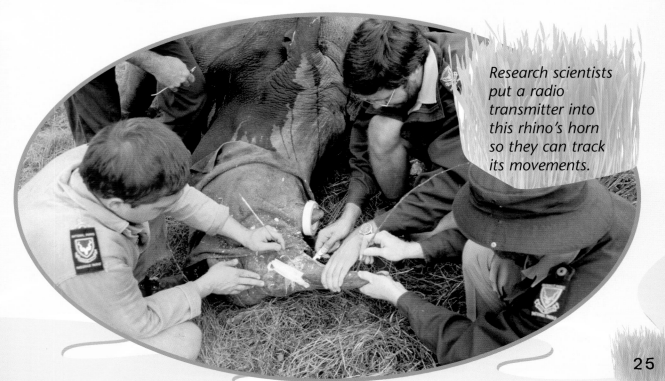

Research scientists put a radio transmitter into this rhino's horn so they can track its movements.

National parks and reserves

National parks and reserves around the world include areas—such as the Serengeti in Tanzania—where grasslands and their wildlife are protected by law. Park workers control who enters the **habitat**. They keep illegal hunters out by guarding animals or by patrolling areas. Tourists are encouraged to visit. The money they pay to get into parks is used to buy equipment and provide jobs, especially for local people. In Namibia, former hunters use their tracking skills to help tourists spot grassland wildlife.

Conservation groups

Conservation groups encourage people to give money and time to protect grasslands by making them aware of the problems grasslands face. For example, the World Wildlife Fund in Australia is helping landowners to control **grazing** and set up reserves in order to protect unusual grassland plants.

Wardens at the Virunga National Park in central Africa go on regular patrols to try and stop poachers from killing elephants for their ivory tusks.

I.Z.C.N.
PARC NATIONAL DES VIRUNGA
UNITE ANTI-BRACONNAGE
ELEPHANT

Research a grassland food web

You can research your own grassland food chains and webs, using information from this and other books, TV programs, and the Internet. Figure out which **organisms** live in a particular grassland. It helps to put them into groups, such as insects, birds, and **mammals**, for example. Then think about their lives:

1. How does the weather affect them?
2. How do they get their food, water, or shelter?
3. What is their role in the grassland—**producer** or **consumer**, **predator** or **prey**?

To make a food chain, it may help to identify the biggest predator and then find out the different prey it eats, what the prey itself eats, and so on, until you get to a plant—the start of the food chain!

You might be able to visit a grassland habitat, like this North American national park, to do your own research!

Where Are the World's Main Grasslands?

This map shows the location of the main grassland **habitats** across the world.

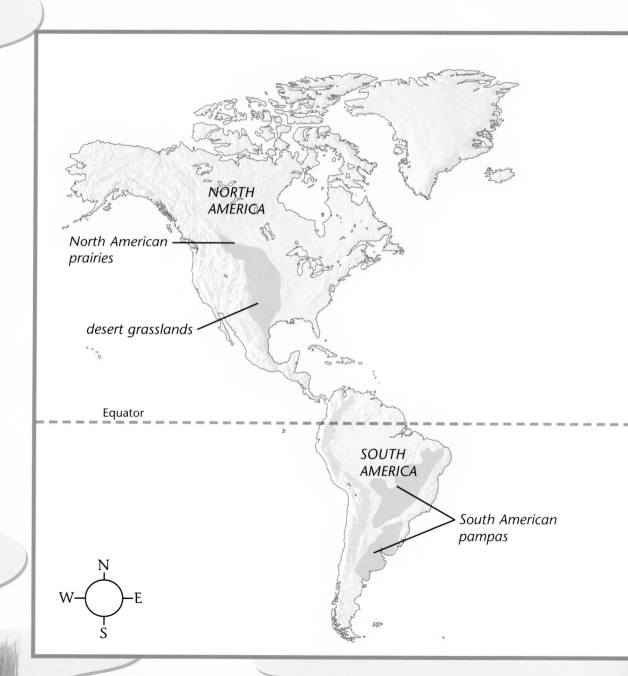

North American prairies

desert grasslands

NORTH AMERICA

Equator

SOUTH AMERICA

South American pampas

N
W — E
S

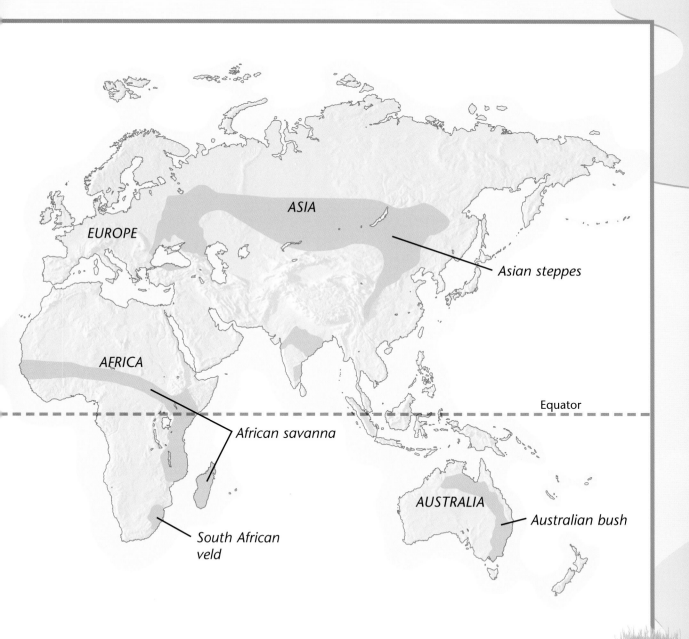

EUROPE

ASIA

Asian steppes

AFRICA

Equator

African savanna

South African veld

AUSTRALIA

Australian bush

Glossary

bacteria (singular bacterium) tiny living decomposers found everywhere

bird of prey bird that hunts animals for food

carnivore animal that eats the flesh of another animal

climate general conditions of weather in an area

conservation protecting and saving the natural environment

consumer organism that eats other organisms

decomposer organism that breaks down and gets nutrients from dead plants and animals and their waste

endangered at risk of dying out completely, as a species of animals or plants

energy power to grow, move, and do things

extinct died out completely

fungi (singular fungus) group of decomposer organisms including mushrooms, toadstools, and their relatives

graze to eat growing grass

habitat place where an organism lives

herbivore animal that eats plants

larvae (singular larva) young of some insects and other animals

mammal animal that feeds its babies on milk from its own body

native belonging naturally to an area

nutrient chemical that plants and animals need to live

omnivore animal that eats both plants and other animals

organism living thing

parasite organism that lives on or within another living thing and feeds from it, without offering any benefit in return

photosynthesis process by which plants make their own food using carbon dioxide (a gas in the air), water and energy from sunlight

pollination when pollen moves or is carried from the male part of a flower to the female part to form seeds

predator animal that hunts and eats other animals

prey animal that is caught and eaten by a predator

primary consumer animal that eats plants

producer organism (plant) that can make its own food

rodent mammal with large gnawing front teeth, such as a mouse or rat

scavenger organism that feeds on dead plant and animal material and waste

secondary consumer animal that eats primary consumers and other secondary consumers

species group of organisms that are similar to each other and can breed together to produce young

temperate belonging to a region of the world that has warm summers and cold, wet winters

tropical belonging to a region of the world that is warm all year round but has one or more rainy seasons

More Books to Read

Baldwin, Carol. *Living in a Prairie*. Chicago, IL: Heinemann, 2003.

Greenaway, Theresa. *Food Chains*. Chicago, IL: Raintree, 2001.

Lauber, Patricia. *Who Eats What?* New York: HarperCollins, 2001.

Patent, Dorothy Hinshaw. *Life in a Grassland*. Minneapolis, MN: Lerner, 2002.

Spilsbury, Louise, and Richard Spilsbury. *Plant Habitats*. Chicago, IL: Heinemann, 2003.

Squire, Ann. *Animal Homes*. Danbury, CT: Scholastic Library, 2002.

Wallace, Holly. *Food Chains and Webs*. Chicago, IL: Heinemann, 2001.

Wallace, Marianne. *America's Prairies and Grasslands*. Golden, CO: Fulcrum Publishing, 2001.

Index